Lorikeet's Encounter Gustav Goanna
Second Edition

Rainbow Lorikeets are so full of life, their fun-loving, mischievous nature is captivating.

This story, the third in the Lorikeet's Book Series for young readers, is based on a family of Lorikeets who encounter an unwanted predator in the garden who takes a genuine interest in them.

Through my words and the creative vision of Lillian Falzon, whose illustrations brought these characters to life, I hope you enjoy a peek into the adventures of this quirky, colourful family.

Lawrence, Loretta and their family of Rainbow Lorikeets are enjoying an afternoon snack of nectar from the blossoms high in the gum trees.

For a treat they fly down from the trees to feast on the sunflower seeds in the garden below.

Their brightly coloured green feathered coats, yellow and red vests and blue headwear glow brightly in the afternoon sun.

The chicks are chattering and flying from tray to tray having a wonderful time, showing off the red lining of their coats and their yellow and green tail feathers.

Lawrence lets out a huge screech. Immediately everyone stops what they are doing and fly into the trees.

Looking down from the safety of the trees, the Lorikeet family can see a very large, prehistoric beast lurching along the ground beneath them.

Looking very suave in his dark grey coat is Gustav Goanna. He has white spots on his skin and grey bands across his back to the end of his very long tail.

The short-sighted Gustav can't see the Lorikeets but is flicking his tongue in and out of his mouth trying to get a scent.

The Lorikeet family are high above in the trees chattering and screeching, watching Gustav, knowing they are out of reach.

Gustav can hear chatter in one of the trees. He lurches toward the noise and begins the steep climb up the trunk.

His very long, razor sharp claws make it easy to hold on.

Laura, Lolita and Lance are in the tree just above Gustav and quickly fly to the tree where their parents, Lawrence and Loretta are.

Gustav searches the tree thoroughly for a nest with 'birds' eggs, his favourite food.

Out of luck, he climbs down the tree and marches along the ground, hissing his displeasure.

Persistent, Gustav climbs up another tree. This time it's the tree where Lawrence, Loretta and the chicks are perched.

Lawrence stands tall, puffs out his red and yellow chest, ruffles his pastel green collar and starts to screech, trying to scare Gustav off.

Gustav, unable to find eggs is determined to make a meal of the brightly coloured Lorikeets.

Lawrence, Loretta, Laura, Lolita and Lance fly into another tree.

Gustav again frustrated, clambers down the tree and stomps along the ground disappointed and decides to sun himself instead.

He climbs along a fallen down tree and stretches himself out in the afternoon sun, takes a deep breath and closes his eyes to replace his energy.

Lawrence whistles to his family it is okay to return to the feeders. His family fly down from the sanctuary of the trees.

In the tree above, Lawrence stays on guard, watching Gustav to make sure his family are no longer in danger.

After a long while Gustav lifts his head, stretches his long body, slides off the log and stumbles off into the undergrowth below the trees.

Lawrence still high in the trees watches Gustav.

He sees Gustav's tail slowly disappearing out of sight and Lawrence has a sigh of relief as he hears him moving further and further away, crunching the leaves under foot.

Now that Lawrence is sure Gustav has moved on and Loretta and his family are safe, he flies down to the garden and joins them.

The Lorikeets now relax and eat the sunflower seeds without fear of the resident Goanna, Gustav, making a meal of them.

Lorikeet's Encounter Gustav Goanna

ISBN

978-1-7640295-5-1 (Paperback)

978-1-7640295-6-8 (eBook)

www.ingramcontent.com/pod-product-compliance
Lightning Source LLC
Chambersburg PA
CBHW060841270326
41933CB00002B/164

9 7 8 1 7 6 4 0 2 9 5 5 1